PRAISE FOR ELI '

"*The Good Arabs* is a beautiful, unflinching book. I love the way conversations become poems, the way 'the past becomes the present when we speak it into existence.' With every sense a body can have, El Bechelany-Lynch invites us to turn toward complexity, to ask questions and never settle for easy answers."

–Tess Liem, author of *Obits* (Gerald Lampert Memorial Award)

"Reading El Bechelany-Lynch, you are reminded to come with tenderness to the work of ordinary things so that something larger and more lasting can begin."

–Canisia Lubrin, author of *The Dyzgraphxst* (Griffin Poetry Prize)

"*The Good Arabs* is an incredibly written collection of poems that explores the Arab identity, the Arab queer identity, through an intersection of conflicting languages and voices. Some poems are conversations with Arabs, other poems are written using Arabic letters, while other poems have words that are Arabic but written using English letters. These highlight the poetic voices that are yearning to find answers in this cultural war with the personal. This beautiful collection asks us to step back, to become a witness, to consider our own histories, the deep roots of our own identities and our desires to be seen in transparency. Eli Tareq El Bechelany-Lynch is an amazing poet and this book is a testament to that. A must read."

–Hasan Namir, author of *War/Torn* & *God in Pink* (Lambda Literary Award)

THE GOOD ARABS

THE GOOD ARABS

Poems

Eli Tareq El Bechelany-Lynch

METONYMY PRESS

Montreal, Quebec

"Do You Run When You Hear the Sound of a Loud Crack?" is a work of fiction. Names, characters, events, and incidents are either the products of the author's imagination or used in a fictitious manner. Any resemblance to actual persons, living or dead, or actual events is purely coincidental.

First edition
First printing - 2021
Printed in Quebec, Canada, by Imprimerie Gauvin
ISBN: 978-1-9990588-9-0 (paperback) | ISBN: 978-1-7774852-0-7 (electronic book)

Metonymy Press
PO Box 143 BP Saint Dominique
Montreal, QC H2S 3K6 Canada

Cover image by Lee Lai; cover design by LOKI
Poetry editing by Trish Salah
Author photo by Laurence Philomène

Some poems in this collection were previously published:

"Reading *Wanting in Arabic*" - *Headlight Anthology*, 19, 2016
ابن - Frog Hollow Press, The City Series #6: Montreal, 2017
"fucked in english" - *The Shade Journal,* Spotlight Issue: Seed, August 2017
"yt people think i'm yt like" - *Plenitude Magazine*, November 2018
"When I lived on Acadie" - *Arc Poetry Magazine*, 90, Fall 2019
"The space between you and us" and "underwater" - *Room Magazine*, 43.2, Summer 2020
"home = garbage" - Watch Your Head, September 2020
"The Good Arabs" - Dusie, Tuesday poem #393, October 2020
"Nancy Ajram made me gay" - *Contemporary Verse 2*, 43.2, Winter 2021
"Who Gives Us The Permission to Exist?" - *carte blanche*, 40, Winter 2021
"The Tradition" and "850 million tonnes" - *smoke and mold*, 4.2, April 2021

We acknowledge the support of the Canada Council for the Arts.
Nous remercions le Conseil des arts du Canada de son soutien.

 Canada Council   Conseil des arts
for the Arts   du Canada

Library and Archives Canada Cataloguing in Publication

Title: The good Arabs : poems / Eli Tareq El Bechelany-Lynch.
Names: Tareq El Bechelany-Lynch, Eli, 1994- author.
Identifiers: Canadiana (print) 20210278765 | Canadiana (ebook) 20210278803 | ISBN 9781999058890 (softcover) | ISBN 9781777485207 (PDF)
Subjects: LCGFT: Poetry.
Classification: LCC PS8639.A735 G66 2021 | DDC C811/.6—dc23

To my mother, the kindest Arab I know

CONTENTS

SECTION THREE: *In the Heart of the Heart of More Garbage*

Nancy Ajram made me gay

Could be a woman. Could be a man. Could be someone floating
in between, or somewhere else, someone in a different country
on a different plane, a different part of Earth's tectonic plates
a space right in between two of them, two men sharing a bed
but no one knows, a shattering
earthquakes so normal we all know the drill
know to keep the good plates strapped in
know that sometimes you wake up to shaking
you wake up to floating
those minutes in between sleep and the shake, endless
until they're not. You're up
and out of the apartment
your pants still hang between your legs. Pull them up
running down the stairs, hoping
no one sees
but someone always does

Could be a woman, could be a man, you never know
with this language, never know
when Arabic holds an inherent femininity between Her lips
between the short I's and the breathy A's
men's mouths filled with feminized verbs
thrown around like hot pita
the air between, the bread swelling, held at the end
of fingertips, hot, crisp, and swollen. Cousins, aunts, uncles yelling
one end of this long table
to the other, voices mingling in one loud white noise
passing plates back and forth, throwing balls of hot pita
bottles of birra
Before gender, still sunken deep into Her language
into hugs, kisses between men
the woman's hand resting on another woman's cheek

I

leaning deeply, looking gently
the moon's wink haunting vast desert nights
the glimmer of the sand sparkling in the light cast
nomadic peoples moving, moving, moving
tectonic plates jerking

I release my femininity in Arabic
move with a body unseen in English
like every time Nancy Ajram comes on, I get up
wriggle my hips and summon my preteen body
writhing to the sounds of the oud
my eyes closing as Nancy's voice guides me
into the crowd of my family
pulling my cousins in to dance
raising my arms, twisting my hips
and emulating Nancy belly dancing in her music video
a shake of the hip for every Akhasmak Ah
hand twist Ah
hip shake Ah
hip shake Asibak La'

SECTION ONE: *Are We Not Arabs?*

Conversations with Arabs

Conversation #1

"What is Phoenicia?"

"It is us."

"But what is us?"

"I do not know."

"Are we Arabs?"

"I was told not."

"By who?"

"I don't know."

"Where does your family come from?"

"They don't know."

"Neither do mine."

"But they say Phoenicia, long ago."

"When is that?"

"I do not know."

"Does she still live on, this Phoenicia?"

"Why is she a woman?"

"Aren't all land masses women?"

"That's transphobic."

"You are right."

"I wrote an essay about it."

"Enough about that now."

"What is a body called when it's suffering? What is the rubble when it's left behind?"

"What?"

"What?"

"Are we not talking about Arabs?"

"Are Arabs not rubble? Are Arabs not suffering?"

"Are Arabs not joy? Are Arabs not singing?"

"Are Arabs not extremists? Are Arabs not dangerous?"

"Are Arabs not diverse? Are Arabs not religious?"

"The buildings are growing higher and higher. The buildings cost too much."

"What buildings?"

"The ones lost in the war."

"The war was so long ago."

"The are many people alive to remember it."

"But can't we forget?"

"But shouldn't we remember?"

Conversation #2
(with a foreigner)

"Have you ever seen garbage piled up so high you cannot see the front entrance of an apartment building?"

"I have only seen garbage in dumps, going on for kilometres."

"Do you think that is a better way?"

"I don't like to see it. I don't like to smell it."

"Is ignorance bliss?"

"We have newer incinerators, newer technologies. They are keeping us safe."

"Who are they?"

They do not speak.

"But you are right, the incinerators we have are old. We do not have a comprehensive solid waste-management strategy."

"What do these words mean?"

"I don't know."

"Then why do you say them to me?"

"I just parody the headlines of news articles."

"It is unsafe."

"I thought you didn't like to see."

"I choose what I like to see."

"There again is the choice."

Conversation #3

"Someone should do something about this!"

"What is 'this'?"

"All of this!"

"You gesture but there is so much it could be."

"I mean everything."

"But who is someone?"

"I'm not sure."

"And why not you?"

"It can't be me."

"Why not?"

"I am so far away."

"Then why don't you go a little closer?"

"I do not want to lose my comforts."

"Ah."

"Ah, what?"

"Isn't it always that?"

home = garbage
for Khalo

looking out the window
    from my teta's balcony
at the news on my laptop
    some days   they look the same
      and some days they don't
    my aunt says, *this is weird*
    there have never been any military tanks
      in zalka before
    three days in a row
imagine the difference between
    this looks weird
    and military men directing traffic
    on a daily basis
rifles slung across their shoulders
    waving the cars to keep going
        stop, turn left
    cars in two lanes somehow
    fitting themselves four wide
    stop, keep going, turn left

this country is corrupt, says my uncle
    this country smells like garbage
contracts with the garbage company left unrenewed
    military men pinching their noses
    while directing traffic
      if we can't manage garbage
      can we do anything right?
    we stop, keep going, turn left

people sling bags of rotten garbage
over mountainsides
over roadsides
drop garbage onto houses
into the ocean
anywhere but garbage disposal
where to dispose
when there is nowhere

four months and my uncle is hospitalized
lungs filled with pollution
hundreds of people in the country
polluted

beirut protesters push
industrial garbage bins
into the middle of the road
try pretending that doesn't exist
at government officials
refusing press
people start to move them
most people drive around them
an obstacle course
in preserving ignorance
let us press it deeper
throw bags over the shoulders of refugees
this country is too small
as though that's the only problem
religion into garbage
brown sludge building

when it's too hot to stay inside
my family heads to the beach
stops at a checkpoint
on the way up the mountains
the military man with a rifle
across his shoulders barely looks
wipes sweat off his brow
bored, nods, motions us forward
the privilege of christianity
there are hundreds of military checkpoints
in this tiny country
hundreds of bored military men
stop, keep going, shmael
there are thousands of palestinians
in refugee camps in this country
stop, undocumented, prohibited
movement hindered
by checkpoints in and out
stop, undocumented, prohibited

I don't live in zalka anymore
but every year I visit
the garbage keeps growing
downtown beirut skyscrapers
hiding the garbage
close the back windows
or we'll smell garbage
speeding on the only highway in lebanon
past garbage piles in flames
taller than the gas station beside it
my uncle's lungs filled with garbage
this country is corrupt, says my uncle
and I ask him why he's still here
it's home, he says, his nose plugged

my family came back eighteen years ago
this is home, they say
lungs filled with garbage

ابن

he sits on a piece
of rock staring up
at the Jupiter temple
in Ba'albek six columns
still
standing

mouldings nearly perfect
facing south
the north faces
worn almost bare by
the Beqaa's winter winds

the sun
making every body
and every thing drip
rivers of sweat
flowing
down their backs
his mother
sitting beside him
moist upper lip says
I swear we have never been closer
to the sun
before today

don't let me be lonely
after Claudia Rankine

she said don't let me be lonely

and i said, lonely? okay.

her meaning i meaningfully obscure

she is probably smarter than me

it's hard to admit as a virgo

i can't tell if you hear what i'm saying

the absence is essentially forgotten

THE ONLY THING ON MY MIND IS FUCK ISRAEL

the only thing i put out into the world is don't talk to me

the only thing i reach for is your hand

if only i had a dollar for every time i hear someone say ay-rab

i would not have many dollars because i don't have tv

i don't live in the states

i don't do many drugs

i did cocaine once, does that count?

those silly people don't know anything about anything

i am silly and don't know anything about anything

if we compare ourselves to those loved by many

we will always get hate on twitter

don't give your opinion too loudly

don't tell them that they're wrong

cancel culture doesn't exist for the privileged

we weigh in on matters far away

keep your six metres away from me

you might not be able to see it

but the only part of my nose that i love

is the part that's bigger than yours

the space between you & us
after Danez Smith's "in lieu of a poem, i'd like to say"

lemon juice squeezed from large bright yellow lemons & garlic cloves pushed
through the garlic press & the bits left inside & stirring the shreds into tahini &
whisking it quickly to thin the hummus & scooped by crunchy bits of pita pieces
cracked & some left in the spread & the movement of my teta's dentures in her
mouth & the gardenia smells wafting outside teta's stone house & little kids running
through parc ex yelling in algerian & the may sun reminding me of life & my khalo
holding me tightly before I board the plane & the 3ammos washing their cars with
laundry detergent & aunties in the hijabs talking quickly arms linked & the wind
blowing you off your bike & the half yellow half green grass & sounds of the morning
prayers waking me up & standing on the small balcony hanging our clothes on the
clothesline & crust of sugar on the rosewater bottle & the white pumpkin seeds spit
out of 3ammo's mouth & the spit-filled bag with spit-coated white shells & being sent
back to canada with so many bags of nuts & the living room only used for guests &
the yes you give when you're really excited & the noes I have to hear & the noes I agree
to & the birth chart we all love to read & calling my mama asking how to translate
"heaven" into arabic & the old lebanese man telling me *I don't understand you young
        people and your tattoos* & the questions on everyone's lips
& the heavy step of your gait   & the weight of a book
in your hands   & the scream sitting
on the edge of teta's lips & & &

                    my teta peels skin off six radishes
            & washes them with bottled water
                            & puts them on the edge of my plate
                                    says *just for you, habibi*

The Tradition
after Jericho Brown's The Tradition

outside, near the depanneur on ogilvy

and hutchison, or close by on querbes and st-roch,
we walk slowly, heads bowed down, out of bed
before we make it to the bend

in the road

this feeling of will they fall out
won't they fall out
like apples at the end

of the season

rotted inside, filled with bees
a thud as they hit the ground

or maybe they aren't falling, a wrap around the chest
what are they if they are not actually there

no apples, no other fruit, the fall a tender season
before the challenge of incoming winter

if not, then what of this feeling of remembering
the absence pretending it is not absence, but something

like the way we cheese at our mom
show brushed teeth, scream *finished*, head off to bed, a minute early

or maybe the way a tree is only a tree if it is filled with lilacs
sometime in early june, the sound of you typing from the kitchen

the only way to remember you're still around, but if not
something deeper, a chant we recite that sounds like it belongs

to church, but it doesn't, a hymn deep in the tongue
rarely spoken by your mother anymore, if only to transition

centuries upon centuries of tradition into now

leaked down the family trees, a sap, perhaps this time, a cedar
or the apple tree on the end of your street, when you finally get home

lie on the couch with your head propped up, and wonder
how did we ever make it back here alive?

Maa al Salama

With age, we become more intimate, something that makes us both sweat
if only we could speak more plainly, instead, we sweat and we sweat

the past becomes the present when we speak it into existence
my khalo tells me about the time he first came to Canada, sweaty

in the way I inherit, nervous in the way I also inherit
he took a boat and then a plane, and then a plane, dripping with sweat

sitting beside an Egyptian man, mouth hard with G. My khalo is kind but distracted
though the conversation gives him some lightness, a little bit of sweet-

ness lingering in the man's mouth after they share chocolate, he looks my uncle up
and down and khalo takes a gulp, his body vibrating with a new kind of nervous sweat

at the security checkpoint, his armpit stains so wet the T-shirt looks
three times as dark, through his grey shirt he sweats and he sweats

staring at the tall back in front of him, he joins one of the lines, praying, Allah y saaedneh
when he looks up finally, he sees a familiar face smiling at him, drying the sweat

Ahlan! the Egyptian man says and my khalo passes him his passport. Barely looking at it
the man passes it back, my khalo replying with a hurried suite

of shoukrans with the most thanks he's ever felt, maa al salama, waves the man
maa al salama says my uncle, his passport and palms dripping with sweat

arguileh breath

children smoke pulls of arguileh too young
sit at the end of the table, hope to grow old too quick

the adults declare the divide from the other side
gossip too loud to be conspicuous

restaurants consumed with music
and lungs sparkling with toufaha-flavoured pulls

a woman stares across, the incarnation of a djinn
bold and beautiful, deep blue dress hanging off her thick body

and they wake with a start, appearing suddenly in the middle of the table
more ethereal than the djinn herself, a woman simply, truly, but for her eyes

spiralling deep into their head, a vision of a person unknown
in a place home but so unknown

but could you secure my heart if I showed you too much, they ask her
but could you know me if I showed you too much, she asks them

at length, a spread across an ocean but
just looking for a way to sustain

any kind of feeling beyond a rush, a stomach spin and swirl
mashed basil leaves and pine nuts, goat cheese and olive oil

hot pita bread rising between an older woman's fingers, her oval rock
body hidden in the corner, pale yellow scarf around her shoulders

the pita thrown onto their plate and they poke the belly
the air release moves through them, a hitch in their throat

fucked in english

the sound is high and loud pitched.
i am the sound.
the sound belongs to the speakers.
i am not the speaker.
my butt on the speaker, vibrating to the sound.

sweat all over my butt cheeks
from the speaker heat, all over my chest
in a binder compress,
thirty-degree weather, i want to show you
something.

the woman with the voice emits
a high-pitched scream, indistinguishable arabic
over the dj set, over the crowd. the woman is
in the speakers.

the woman makes noises impossible in english
and i am watching her.
the lights are dim at this party.
the man with the too-loud and too-vocal voice walks by.
only one of him in this room, thank dog.

there are two of us.
i am sipping a beer, talking about letting you
through my beer-soaked happiness and you follow
me around the room.
we are easily circulating, despite the thick crowd.
in this smushed sweat basin.
my ears brim filled with your voice despite small ear canals.
because we are close enough.
i lean in so i don't say what so much.

i am as sober as i want to be, and feeling as attractive
as my beer-soaked brain will tell me.
i still feel insecure. when i have no more secure
to hold me, i let you hold for a bit.

the air is sweat and beer.
the air is thick and indistinguishable arabic.
i am fucked.
the message is good luck.
i am the good. i remind myself.
you are the luck.

i can't find the message hidden
under her speakers.
the woman now screeching
the woman is in arabic
the woman, piercing.
you ask me, what is the woman saying?
i tell you. the woman is saying she's fucked.

Who Gives Us the Permission?

Dear God, if only you knew the sound
coming out of my mouth
was pleasure not pain, if only,
how the ways we touch each other
can be both. The scramble to decide who we are
originated not so long ago. If words mean something,
then choosing holds all the power. Flesh is flesh is flesh
hanging off the cross. They say he was alive, skin and bones,
tendons, fat, until he wasn't, and then, well,
he was hanging on my mother's
living room wall.

Flesh is flesh is flesh
when it's dead. Alive, it is skin and bones and smiles
and slaps and foreign and loved and close
and new and perishable and hurt and the redness of standing out
in the cold with not much on. Stab me in the back,
why don't you?

The trust we feel
has been given to us by holy men
who treat children like playthings
and women like vessels. Don't stop there,
we must criticize and criticize
with an openness like the potholes in Montreal.
Saying one thing and meaning another
has not led us anywhere. Speak the truth, they say
but what is the truth
when we're all holding on
to something different? What is the truth
when the lies we tell ourselves
help us sleep at night?

It was

It was a rip and a heart and a sleeve but not in that order.

It was a stage and a fight and an act but not in that order.

Set the stage for the things you want to see happen to you, something like positive thinking.

Leaving is an option   Staying is another

The man yelling on the other side of the road screams we have no real options, sees me through Parc Ex darkness, do you want to buy some weed?

E tells me they admire my ability to say yes but it's because I can't say no.

I think I'm a happy person until I'm not.

I think I'm a valuable person until I'm not.

The space between my options and yours is the distance between Vancouver and Montreal. This is not a metaphor, this is physical.

We joke about swapping out everyone we don't like in this city for everyone we love living elsewhere. The list grows longer and longer until we have to stop, heavy. Montreal is a transitional city. I'm still here.

The space between my irritation and theirs is the length of my body.
I hold it inside, a rupture, a case of internal bleeding.
We must keep it contained, safe, locked.

The scene is a recurring one. The sky is darkening, deep purples and soft pinks bruising, we are bruising, waiting for the marks to heal, soft skin returning to olive.
Your bite marks my shoulder before you leave.

We pick fruit from the olive trees, send pictures home to friends, ripen in the sun.

My love, says the main figure on the stage,
I only miss you when I'm lonely and that isn't often.

We count the months between Montreal and Lebanon, the distance is ten snowfalls and hundreds of coffees poured and shrinking.

My cousin tells me a man is a man and a woman is a woman after taking one look at me.

We read books in the sun side by side. You read a passage that makes you frown, but when I ask you what's wrong, you ignore me, reading.

Two bodies never fall asleep at the same time.

The distance between whiteness and race is the Atlantic Ocean and the Pacific Ocean and the Gulf of Mexico and the Mediterranean Sea.

The distance between whiteness and brownness is my movement.

The distance between my whiteness and my brownness is vague.

We are onstage, painting our nails silver glitter. I wave my hands up and down to dry. You tell me I look like a slow-motion hummingbird.

He tells me, people here keep asking me if I'm in process (transition).

He says, I have so many stories to tell you.

I tell him, people always look at me as though I'm in process (transition). People are looking for my ends, my stops. I fail to tell them I don't have any.

We spend hours venting. We are always venting.

The closing scene is sitting around the table, trying positive thinking.
We hum, we listen to a tape of Cher, we close our eyes.

The closing scene is you telling me to get into bed, you rolling over,
you looking away then back, you making the first move, you working up the courage to
say—

The closing scene is a group of queers bursting into laughter, sides split.

It was a stitch and a burst and a side but not in that order.

Grey

The building is grey, the sidewalk, grey
the tarp over the banana trees, also grey

but the bananas? They are green until they are not
but of course it's still early in the season

The smell of garbage wafts up to the fourth floor
of Teta's building, her apartment shut off

from the outside during the day. We also smell air conditioning
the particular tinge of cold air; the covers never hold me

tightly enough. I wake up in the arctic bedroom
throw the door open and rush to the bathroom

and shit for hours. When my stomach feels empty
the kind of lurching you feel when there's nothing left to puke

the water that exits my asshole continues to take on
a brown tinge. The bathroom is brown

the tree trunk outside the windows, brown
the sofas we aren't supposed to sit on? They are brown too

wrapped in plastic wrap and my body, the lurch in my stomach
settled enough to fall asleep in plus-forty heat

you're mistaken! I didn't drink the contaminated water
never from the sink, no, nor the shower

brushed my teeth and never swallowed.
The water is, but maybe, no, the ice?

The restaurant served me ice, yes, but they wouldn't, no
from the tap? Was it the AC that put me in that state

but who knows? The water has been contaminated
since the days of oh I don't know. Sweat runs

down my inner arms, liquid turning my shirt yellow. Why, I ask,
does the right armpit always smell worse than the left?

850 million tonnes

months of garbage into the sea, 850 million tonnes
     last week, it rained in the city of Beirut, locals woke up to a river of trash
   slithering between their houses   it's going into your sea?
             it's washing back up   onto your beaches?
how awful this garbage, *the collection company contract ended*, it's all free governance,
corruption, mismanagement   it's all garbage-filled streets
            the old man on the side of the road, yelling they threw it into our sea
        · to no one   scooters speeding by on small cobble streets
    building an incinerator from scratch   a separation of garbage at the source
a second separation   a treatment of garbage and recycling
    but what type   what standards
what generation of incinerators   new filters?   old beat-up Mercedes speed by
   large puffs of smoke leaving behind   grey air
     the kids on the side of the road begging   for better lungs
       hands grey-brown with dust

he says it requires continuous filtration
          but our government is not trustworthy

they hold so many solutions   nonactionable
     without the incinerator   waste management can still happen
when burning everything   the rest   where is it gonna go
     matter doesn't just disappear   trapped in the air
     in the lungs of old women   on the coats of feral cats
in the skin of bananas   infused in the oil of kahwa
     Lebanese citizens already ahead of the government
     many neighbourhoods recycle on their own expense
     if there are incentives and trust   *many people are ready*
we are always conscious of the danger of the situation
isn't that the Lebanese way
to sort your problems without relying
on your government?

     it's a postmodern state, he says to the foreign reporter on the radio
     we know how to live without the state
and yet fear coats his next words   *within all this*
     Beirut is still charming   *a very hospitable city*
     please don't stop visiting   tourists line the beaches
rushing away in disgust   British accents less and less present

he explains: *low-rise buildings demolished*   *replaced with luxury residential towers*
     owned by Lebanese expatriates   *or foreigners*
     often occupied only seasonally
     fleeing their migrant countries
     for a small whiff of garbage
the expert on the radio   do not forget him   urges   top of his lungs now
like many problems we've gone through
     there will always be a solution   weakly, he promises
     and we citizens are ready to fight for the basics
     the civil movement is very well united
     and working hard
     we are united
     no matter religion
     or political affiliation

We Are Not at Home Here

You sit in the country of your oppression. I, visitor, sit in the country I call home. It's complicated. Neither of us is at home here. Neither of us is foreign. Men look at me like a melting piece of milk chocolate, lighter, filled with almonds, something to crack in half, look inside of. They look at you the same way but you don't notice. We understand staring differently, though you are not so strange, not so queer. When I go back home, I find it dull, lacking fresh bananas and jasmine. I find at home the weightlessness of the English language, though I write it daily, speak it daily, mix in words of French here and there as I climb the bus. I find comfort in the glares here, they have less weight. They have seen many like me here, though a glare is a glare and maybe I still don't feel safe. When we send video messages on WhatsApp, you say you went to the protests, and people leaving told you they were being tear-gassed, to avoid going in. You and your friend entered and inevitably got tear-gassed. The Montreal police are on very friendly terms with tear gas. We are in different places but we are not. I video message you words of comfort and you say, it is just the windows that are shattered, and Teta, she is a bit shaken up.

& if my people

we are but one people & yet so many, formed by nations & variations on the same language & a commitment to being light & a subjugation of people darker than us & yes you may judge us & yes you should & yes look at yourselves too & yes the sounds mix in with the oud & the awh & the shaking of a wrist with heavy bracelets & if my people do this they could do anything & we are better & we are wiser & so we think & so we are wrong & the energy it takes to fight across a table about the importance of human life is disastrous & yet we must do it & yet we must try & yet the times I've fought have unleashed, out of me, a storm & you always say western like it's a bad word & I always say western like it's a bad word & yet we don't mean the same thing & you imply gay rights and Black liberation & I imply colonialism & racism & so on and so forth & around & around until an explosion hits & somehow our conversations stop midsentence & yet when we are the ones starving, we suddenly & only give a shit

The Cycle

1.

these days, I see capitalism written plainly in every poem, though the poetry masters say *show, don't tell*, but if we were to show this indiscernible void, the make-believe of pieces of paper, sometimes coin, that make the world go, not round, but into the hands of the few, would this change how you see this intoxication with power?

2.

he looks up from his food, a hamburger between two slices of bread, and asks as though this were the most important question, *will Teta have enough khoboz to eat back home?*

3.

article 534 of the Lebanese Penal Code prohibits having sexual relations that are "contradicting the laws of nature," which is punishable by up to a year in prison. as a practical matter, enforcement of the law has been varied and often occurs through occasional police arrests.

that is to say, this law was put in place by the French government in the early 1900s.

they say a relic.

I say a shift in the century, a matter of public privacy.

she says *aaybeshoum*, which means, we have absorbed their respectability.

4.

these days, I see more people looking for work. it is unavailable. those of us in the service industry must risk our lives or risk our lives. there is never really a choice. one way or another, they will ultimately claim us. who are they? we don't even know. the facelessness makes them undetectable.

5.

I marvel at the care I find in my neighbours, in my friends, in the people on the internet tweeting dark jokes that sustain me through another day. this weakness in us, in you, in me, is not weakness but a sickness, not always of our own making. we try our best to help each other, but they do not let us. tents are destroyed. shelters must be sober. the snow falls for the first time, and though the streets glimmer white, it is not a good omen.

6.

one day there is money, the next there is not. the value plummets though the pieces of paper still look the same, the lira sitting in my old wallet, hidden away.

7.

the riots begin, a consequence of so much death. it only makes sense. we debate whether this is the right recourse or not. this is not up for debate. what is the difference between objects and people? when we turn certain people into objects, we become monsters, ugliness seen not in the way we look, but in our hearts, drying up yellow, quickly. redirect our attention.

8.

the death of one political man means nothing. i would say woman or person, but it is almost always a man. they replace one man with another, and it is always the same. this time it is in our faces. escalated, some of us adapt. the men are starving, but not for food. this insatiable hunger leaves us wanting for more.

9.

but what is a homosexual who is not a homosexual outdoors, not indoors, not in private? but what is an Arab who is not a homosexual who is not an Arab who is not a homosexual?

read: you may only transition if you have the surgery.

that is to say, you must become one of us.

10.

read: a year in prison, read: the police are called, read: the bars are raided, read: acts "contradicting the laws of nature," read: at the hands of the police, read: and the military.

read: I will not describe to you what violations occur, what a prison looks like, if only to stop the violence from reoccurring on the page.

SECTION TWO:
Do You Run When You Hear the Sound of a Loud Crack?

Conversations with Arabs

Conversation #4

"What about the good Arabs?" you ask.

"What would I know about good Arabs?"

"Is it not the title of your book?"

"Oh. That."

"Yes, indeed. Are you, oh holy one, calling yourself a good Arab?

You, who has the power over the words in this book?"

I try, "Of course I don't think I am good.

Okay, so that is a lie.

My greatest weakness is my ego."

"Is this vulnerability?" you ask.

I say, "No, this is what choice looks like.

I pick and choose what to share."

"Why talk about goodness when this idea of good is fraught?"

"I am trying to figure it out for myself."

"So you don't know the answers?"

"I do not."

"Then why write a book?"

"I am searching."

Conversation #5

"I'm sick of hearing white people talk about bombs."

"Now you've caught my attention."

"And trivializing our lives. The lives of our families."

"Yes! Now we've got something in common. Keep speaking."

"The Arab world is more than war."

"We have our food!"

"No, that isn't it either. You know how much they love hummus."

"I saw chocolate hummus in the grocery store the other day."

"No!"

"And Israeli falafel on the corner of my street."

"Falafel isn't Israeli."

"You should tell THEM that."

"I will. Will you come with me?"

"No."

"How come?"

"I accidentally bought some from there yesterday."

"What do you mean, accidentally?"

"Well, it is Arab owned."

"I thought Israelis owned it."

"They do. They are Palestinian. But also Israeli…"

"Oh."

"Yes."

"Well that's complicated."

"Isn't it?"

Conversation #6

"Play Fairouz."

"No, I want to listen to Oum Kalthoum."

"Not this evening. What about Dalida?"

"La'. How about Sabah?"

"Oof, no no. Let's listen to Nagat El-Sagheera?"

"Who is she? Khalas, I've figured it out. Do you have any Abdel Halim Hafez records?"

"Oh no no. I only listen to women."

"How come?"

"The diva is the centre of the Arab world."

Do You Run When You Hear the Sound of a Loud Crack?

Mar Elias Church - 2040

The church is alive with Teta's wails and she leads us into our mourning. She is in the centre of the first row, and her cries fill the space, bouncing off the glass windows. I pinch the thin flesh of my wrist to help me hold in my tears. I haven't been to church in ages. My body is stiff, and I try to move a little bit without sticking out. I rub at my shoulders that hurt more than usual as I try to stand tall and straight. I avoid eye contact with my countless relatives, their gazes filled with pity.

Eventually, the priest starts chant-singing. I sit three rows behind my teta but her grief consumes me, consumes the church, clings to the walls, to the stained glass, becoming part of the architecture. If I squint and look at the light in just the right way, shining through the glass painting of an angel with its arms lifted upwards, I can see the dust particles, sense the layers of grief years old, hear the sobs of other tetas years ago, decades ago, many conflicts ago. My teta's wails join the priest's chants and together they make music. My younger sister Najwa slips her hand into mine. I don't turn towards her but the warmth steadies me a little. She cries softly, her body shaking.

In the most recent round of killings, after the most widespread protests in the country, sixty-five people were killed, including five children caught in the crossfire. My khalo, Teta's eldest, among the dead. Trying to help children caught in a bombed building, he did not survive the attack, another bomb landing on that same building, exploding, shattering, killing anyone who didn't die from the first blow. Most of us don't believe the government, their attempts to blame the deaths of the most prominent leftist rebel group, disillusioned as we are by decades of of empty commitments to change, government aid that never came, hospitals never erected, hungry mouths never fed. I look up, an ache, my breath hard to steady. I breathe deeply many times to return it to its normal rate, trying to calm my heart at the same time.

Could one person's death be more important than those of hundreds at the hands of our government?

Though the casket is empty, my khalo's body unreachable under rubble, I see him in the golden dust, in the sunlight leaking into the church, hear him in my teta's sobs. My khalo is gone, and so are his glistening brown eyes, his tenderness, his anger only unleashed when pushed, his secretive life, his young years spent in the war. My khalo is dead and for today, I hold space only for this singular grief. Tomorrow I will grieve my country.

I drift off when the classic Arabic of the priest becomes too hard to understand, the chants becoming background noise. My hand is numb in Najwa's. I haven't moved it enough throughout the ceremony. When the priest guides us to our knees, I return to my body and worry about having to get back up, my knees aching on the padded cushion. Everyone in the church bows their heads but I keep mine raised, watching.

One of my second cousins is in the row to the left of mine, body rigid, back stiff. I remember the stories of how he mistreated my khalo growing up, calling him names, questioning his sexuality. Staring at him, I don't realize everyone is getting up until Najwa pokes me. She helps me up, notices my knees catching, but I shrug her off. Hard enough not drawing attention as the only queer person in the building. I can't stand receiving condolences, so I shoulder my way towards the exit, leaving Najwa to tend to our mother.

I push past everyone headed to the Aaza. I avoid the looks on their faces. They probably think I'm rude for leaving. Something brushes against my arm and I peer up to see a woman with dark curly hair, a loose headscarf, and dark brown skin touching my arm.

"Allah yirhamo," she says, and before I can look at her closely, she slips back into the crowd and disappears, leaving a scent of jasmine behind. Outside the church, the late morning sun shines, oddly red for this time of day.

Chadi, who had been sitting a few rows away, follows me out of the church.

"Where are you going?"

"The souk, I think. I need a walk, maybe pick up some fruit?"

Chadi tags along, and we walk in silence for a bit.

"Do you want to talk about it?"

"Not at all," I reply, and he grabs my hand, stroking the top with his thumb.

Souk

The cars kick up dust but thankfully I have my sunglasses. I put on my brown leopard

Browlines. Chadi, who is myopic, is safe from the dust attack.

The day is hot, and we turn onto the market street. I take off my dress shirt, sweat so heavy it's soaked the armpits and back. Chadi keeps his on and I wonder how he deals with the heat. His body seems less coated in sweat.

When we arrive at the souk, we head straight to my favourite vendor, Yousef. His akidineh are always the cheapest, and I get a dozen since they're Teta's favourite fruit. I don't realize Chadi isn't beside me until I hear him screaming "Shaheed!"

"Ya zalameh!" he shouts even louder, trying to get his cousin Shaheed's attention across the souk.

I walk up to Chadi and elbow him. "Just walk over to him instead of screaming. It'll be much easier, you know."

"You don't have to come with me. You can just wait here. I won't be long. I know you're not in the mood to talk."

"It's fine. I'll be fine."

Chadi raises his eyebrow but starts walking over to Shaheed, who is holding a bag of mishmish. "How are you, habibi?" Chadi cups his cousin's cheek in his hand, leans in, and gives Shaheed three kisses. Shaheed is in his early thirties, and yet he has deep bags under his eyes, his hair is missing small patches, and he shows signs of greying. He didn't look as worn out a few months ago. I also kiss Shaheed in greeting and notice he's lost weight as I touch his waist.

"I'm okay, Chadi. Kifak inta?"

Shaheed answers our questions with a word or two, lacking his normal enthusiasm. When he turns to me again he looks more like himself for a second.

"I'm sorry, Mo, I heard about your khalo. Allah yirhamo."

"Thank you, Shaheed."

"When I lost my father last year—well—it was one of the hardest periods of my life. I would not wish that on anyone." His eyes glass over and he once again looks much older. I have never heard him speak about his father's death.

He fidgets with the bag of mishmish, twirling it clockwise and then counterclockwise. "I got this fruit for my mother. They're her favourite." I wonder at the change in direction, but then he continues: "My father used to bring her mishmish every Friday. I guess I took over when he passed."

He starts twirling the bag faster. I can feel his anxiety rising in the air between the two of us, and for a second, I forget Chadi is standing here with us. Shaheed starts looking around furtively, between the stands, at his bike, then back at us. I ask, "Are you in a rush, Shaheed? We don't want to keep you."

"No, no, I'm just a little dehydrated. I should head home before I get sunstroke. I forgot to bring water with me."

Before Chadi or I can offer him a bottle, he rushes away, jumping onto his motorbike and riding off.

Zalka

Two days later, I sit on the balcon with Najwa, my teta, my cousin Rose, my aunt, and my mother. There's never been enough room for us all living at my teta's apartment, but somehow we've made it work these past few years. The heat is thick and the power has gone out again so we can't turn on any of the fans or the AC. While I am cooling down by sweating, a slow trickle of water sliding down my face, the others moan and complain, my mother fanning herself dramatically. I look over to Teta and her eyes are vacant.

The curtains are drawn to block the sun, but in the absence of glass panes, they do little to keep the heat out. After the 2020 explosion, Teta couldn't afford to fix the shattered windows. Ours match those of thousands of buildings in the country. International aid didn't last any longer than the news cycle.

Rose brings a bucket of water for Teta's swollen feet. "Shoukran habibti," Teta says. She reaches for her wooden prayer beads lying on the small table beside her and starts humming softly, though not with her usual vigour. Is she starting to doubt the power of prayer? She lost her husband and brother in the Civil War and then her son in the recent government retaliation. If she still has any faith, it is left over from the engravings the nuns of her youth gave her, a habit deeper than belief.

We keep on as we usually do. I wonder how long the ceasefire will last this time. While we wait for things to get bad again, we pray if we are religious, we count the food, we groom the garden, we check in on everyone in the building, we offer meals to Hasmik, the older Armenian woman who lost her family long ago.

As Teta soaks her feet and Rose spits out the shells of pumpkin seeds, we are propelled out of our seats by a whistling sound followed by a blast reverberating against the mountains, its echo reaching us in waves. Water splashes out of Teta's bucket, spraying the tiles and creating puddles around her. When nothing follows the noise, most of us relax, except for Teta, whose shoulders are almost at her ears. She runs to her room, and I know she will return with the hidden whiskey. It's going to be a bad night for everyone.

It isn't long before the shouting begins from her room, before the insults that often follow her Sunday drinks start flying.

"Yekhreb beitkoun," she screams. "Allah yirhamkoun kilkoun. Baladi, ya baladi, weynik?"

"Teta, stop screaming at us from your room!"

"Shoo qilto?" she yells, and her voice is formidable, steady and sharp. I flinch, and almost retreat, but I am not in the mood for mourning the rotting husk of our nation, brown and damp, easy to pull apart, moist on the inside.

The rest of my family stares at me, no longer chewing their pumpkin seeds, mid-fan, eyes narrowing. No one dares to treat Teta so dismissively because we should respect our elders.

"You know it's better off for us if she just stays in her room," I remind Rose. Her face tightens and her pupils narrow.

"Wallow, she's our teta."

"Give it a break," Najwa speaks up for the first time today.

"They aren't a child." She looks at me. "You're in your thirties. You aren't a bratty teen anymore."

"Being an adult doesn't mean taking shit from your elders and holding your tongue. If we're going to talk about childlike behaviour—"

"Bas, bas," echo my mom and my aunt. Then quiet fills the room, unbearable, and no one says anything as I get up and leave.

Jal el Dib

"How are you doing today?"

"Oh you know, Teta is having a hard time, my khalo is dead, just the usual."

Chadi rolls his eyes. "You know, you can just say you're sad." He puts his hand on my shoulder.

I flinch and pull away. I can't tell if he's hurt or just confused. "Let's sit on the balcony," I tell him, and he follows me outside. We melt into the wicker outdoor chairs and I reach for the half bottle of water from the side table and gulp it all down. "The government is giving out rations again," I say, putting the bottle back down.

"Where?"

"In Beirut, of course."

Chadi's thick eyebrows scrunch together, creating a unibrow. "They just want to take some good pictures for the newspapers, make it seem like they're doing something."

"Guess they have to get more creative now that most people aren't able to watch the news on TV. They seem to be learning from the activists."

"Just what we need, a corrupt government with new tactics."

"Honestly, I wish there was an easy solution to all of this." I sigh. "Sometimes you talk like you haven't lived here your whole life, Chadi, like one of those diaspora kids."

"I've seen as much as you have of the corruption of this fucking place. I just wish people didn't have to suffer so much—we didn't have to suffer so much."

I look to the ground, the balcony tiles cold on my bare feet.

"I'm sorry, Mo, I didn't mean to—"

"It's fine. I think I need to lie down, though. My back is killing me." I try to twinkle my eyes in a way that seems seductive. "And maybe we can make out?"

"Every time you say you want to make out, it makes me overthink things. It's not spontaneous."

"My uncle just died," I pout, but I don't have it in me to commit.

"That makes me want to make out even less."

"For some of us, sex is a coping mechanism."

"For some of us, death makes us too sad for sex."

"Okay, okay, let's just cuddle then."

He releases a relieved sigh. "Merci."

"Tikram aainak."

He kisses me on the forehead and we head to the room to lie down. As soon as we get into bed, I fall asleep.

Something is shaking and it might be me. I'm groggy, in that space between dreams and awake, asleep in the eyes, but aware of something changing. Another earthquake? I open my eyes and realize it's Chadi.

"Habibi, there's someone at the door. They said something about Shaheed. You know I don't always understand dialects. Come, please!"

"Who?" I yawn, and my legs are stiff. I can't imagine getting out of bed, but when I blink and rub my eyes, I notice Chadi's contorted face.

"They didn't say their name. They just mentioned something that involved Shaheed?"

Shaheed? I slip my feet into my shifata and get up slowly, Chadi helping me. I do a stretch to remind my legs they are awake and extend my arms over my head, feeling my back muscles contract and extend, not quite relaxed.

"Hello?" I say to the person at the door, who is tall, with a large nose and one long dark braid running down their back. "Do we know each other?" I ask. The person glows a little bit, something about them slightly off. Despite this feeling, I am calm in their presence. The late-afternoon sun shines in through the window in the hallway and imbues them with golden-red sunlight, their light brown skin ablaze.

Chadi fidgets, clicking two nails together, and stares at the stranger.

"Never you mind, dear. You have to go find Shaheed. He is lost, in the downtown. Something is not right."

"What is going on?" Chadi asks, worried now.

"I cannot say, but I must leave you now."

"Wait," I yell. "Who are you?" But they don't respond to my question and disappear. I shake my head. Where have they vanished to? The sun is shining so bright through the windows now that it is hard to see.

"Chadi, did you see where they went?" I ask, squinting a little and turning away from the door.

"I'm not sure. But they must have just run down the stairs."

"How do you think they know Shaheed?"

"I'm not sure," he says again, "but we have to go find him."

"Go find him? You're going to believe some random person's story about Shaheed?

Someone we don't even know?"

"Mo, it's not—"

"There seemed something off about them. What if they're leading us on a wild goose chase?"

"Mo, I think—"

"I think I've seen them somewhere. Do you think they've been following us?"

"Mo, really, I just really think that—"

"And how did they know that we knew Shaheed?"

"Mo, stop! Will you listen to me for a second? Everyone knows each other. Does it matter? I think we need to go. What if he's in danger?"

"So you're just going to launch yourself into the fire unprepared?"

"Oof," he breathes out. "He's my cousin, Mo. Wouldn't you go right away if it was Rose? I'll just go by myself."

"Wait, Chadi!" I grab at his arm and force him to stay. "Wait! You're right. I'll come with you." As much as I don't want to go, something else is telling me we should. I'm not sure if I'm just groggy from sleep, but the stranger's appearance destabilized me. It wasn't just that they were extremely beautiful. Did I know them from somewhere?

In a few minutes, we're hopping onto my motor scooter. I've been saving gas for emergency occasions, for days I can't avoid going far. It is dusk, the golden hour is at its most golden. The sky is split horizontally in half, a dim blue meeting deep orange, and Chadi's skin a brilliant brown. He wraps his arms around me, his dark arm hairs standing up and tickling my exposed skin. We slide around the winding roads, too small to accommodate more than one car. I pass cars quickly, slipping between them, honking and driving aggressively, the only way you can drive in Lebanon, and Chadi holds on tighter, screeching occasionally, screaming at me to slow down, but I laugh and ignore his instructions.

It is almost dark by the time we arrive in Beirut. I wonder how we're ever going to find him in the large capital. I zoom around the downtown area, among the tall skyscrapers and Ottoman-era beige stone buildings with terracotta roofs, a relic from the 1920s. Most of the buildings, new or old, are gutted and shattered, windows just giant holes in the walls, stripped to their basic elements. Closer to where the explosion took place, the city is a gravesite, the leftover parts of the buildings tombstones of a past existence, of a different life. Many people became homeless during the explosion of 2020, and many still roam the streets, though others must have gone off to seek shelter as the night sets in.

I look at Chadi and sigh. "Where do we even start?"

Chadi jumps off the bike. He crosses the narrow road, grabbing the shoulder of a middle-aged man, grey haired and skinny, holding a large bag of rice. "Izah samaht, Monsieur," Chadi says. "Do you know where they are giving out rations?"

He points us in the direction of the Nejmeh Square Clock Tower, one of the buildings that survived the Civil War and one of my favourites. The tourists stopped visiting, the rich fled for the mountains, and the businesses all closed down, except for smaller merchants. The parliament nearby is still occupied, however.

When we arrive, Shaheed is in the middle of the square, his tall body slim, his overgrown red hair bright, surrounded by people. They seem to envelop him as the crowd grows and moves. It is hard to see where he stops and they begin. "What's he doing?" I yell to Chadi over the rumble of my motorbike. I don't hear Chadi's response as we zoom by, trying to cut around people, but I feel him tense up, his arms around me tighter, his back straighter. "Shaheed!" he cries, but the square is too loud, and he doesn't hear us. We are too far away to see his face. As we get closer, we see him pushing through, no longer a piece of the crowd, but parting the waves of people, a force amid the sea. Chadi and I get off the bike, leaving it against a closed restaurant, and start running.

We're a few metres away when we finally notice the general, a tall man heightened by the ledge he stands on, right in front of the clock tower, handing out bags of rice and water bottles. I don't see his bodyguards until I notice them passing him the items to give out. He smiles a perfect celebrity smile, and the people are so hungry, they eat him up, pushing each other to get a bit of food. We can't hear him but we see his hand waving, appeasing the crowd. He might be saying "Bas, bas, there's enough for everyone," though the need is always greater than the supplies in Beirut.

I speed up, yelling at people to move, but we can't seem to catch up. Shaheed is quick, on some kind of mission, heading for the general. The closer he gets, the more his body shakes. Even though I don't know what is happening, there's something about the way his body vibrates that makes me run faster towards the warning of Shaheed's red hair.

We almost reach Shaheed and he is now standing directly in front of the general.

The crowd seems to sense something, and together, they all step back a little. We are a few feet away when we hear the general say, "Ahlan ya zalameh, can't you wait your turn?" And then a gun is out of Shaheed's pocket. I hear a sharp, loud sound, a crack as the bullet breaks the sound barrier, a thump of the round being fired. It echoes through the square and it's hard to tell where it came from. The crowd screams, the crowd roars, the crowd starts running away. I look to the general and he seems okay. It is Shaheed that falls, and I have to stop myself from closing my eyes. The men around the general become more evident, the men are quick, the men are large and commanding. The general is swept away—whisked inside a car that pulls out of nowhere.

Only minutes between the gunshot and now, Shaheed's body is on the ground, leaking dark blood out of his head. The men are gone, the general is gone, and the crowd is now so thin, it barely looks like one.

Chadi immediately splays himself on the ground, touching Shaheed, shaking him, screaming for help, giving up. He is sobbing and I'm just waiting for this moment to end. If I keep standing still, it might not be real. We stay there for what feels like hours, the shock sedating me. I move close to Chadi and say, "Yallah, we have to go," as the men return. The men are large, the men are one, the men are pushing Chadi off Shaheed. The men say, "Are you friends with this traitor?" and the men say "You must leave or else" and the men say "This is a matter of national security."

Chadi doesn't seem to hear them, lying on Shaheed, and I pull on him, saying "Come, habibi, please, habibi, we have to go, habibi."

Chadi shakes his head. "No, please no." The men are pulling on Chadi, the men are moving him, the men are trying to arrest him.

"La', aamilou maarouf," I tell them, and something in one of them ignites, his eyes, almost black and softer than the others', look less resolute, so I bury deeper into what I've found. "I will take him home now, please, we will leave."

The man with dark hair and a short-cropped beard, the one with the eyes, nods, says "Yallah," waves his hand at us, and I am leading Chadi away, sunken, defeated.

I help him onto my bike and wrap his arms around me, say "Hold on tight" and wait until he does. "You have to hold on," I repeat, and we speed away. Shaheed is still on the ground and the men are surrounding him. The men are so tall we can no longer see him.

We pass by some of the same buildings we noticed before. A skyscraper, all glass, thirty storeys tall, reflects the setting sun. The building has never looked as pretty as it does now, casting the sunlight onto the apartment building near it, shorter, six storeys of old stone, brown with dirt, mould, some greenery growing out of the cracks between the stones. We drive on cobblestone narrow streets, passing a vendor selling kaak from his small kiosk attached to a bicycle. He yells at us, probably imploring us to buy something, but we pass him by too quickly. The kaak probably wouldn't be soft enough to eat, hardened from a full day outside. Chadi, suddenly alert, asks, "Where are we going?"

"The beach."

He puts his head against my back, nodding into my dark shirt.

We get onto the highway and the traffic is less thick now that it's dark. Most people are at home, having supper or playing cards. In minutes, we're pulling off the highway, and I head down another narrow road, this time uneven asphalt, avoiding all the potholes. The sea is dark blue, almost black, the waves crashing hard against nearby rocks, the wind stronger as the sky grows darker. Chadi and I get off my bike, stand by the water, and listen to it coming closer to us, then moving back. I take off my shoes and, avoiding the heaps of plastic bottles and chip wrappers on the shore, move closer to the water and stick my feet in, not thinking about how dirty it is. I can't see Chadi but I don't think he's moved, standing behind me with his arms crossed. When I look back, he is looking away, watching the sky darken more with every minute. The waves crash against a nearby rock but I can still hear the sobs in his chest.

When I turn back to the beach, a figure materializes, tall, handsome, and muscular with thick facial hair and a vague glow.

I jump, heart pounding, and turn to Chadi for help, but he is still looking away, not seeming to notice our new companion.

"He doesn't see me," the stranger explains, and I turn back to face him.

"Who are you? And why can't he see you?"

"I'm only showing myself to you. He's so out of it though, poor dear, he doesn't seem to realize you're speaking to someone."

I stare hard, my heart slowed a little bit, but not totally. "Why do you look so familiar?"

"We've met before. Earlier today. And on the day of the funeral."

"I've never seen you before."

"Yes you have, I've just changed form. First, I was the hijabi woman at the church. Then, the femme visiting you at Chadi's. And now, this man," he adds, pointing to himself for dramatic effect. "Now, dear, can you guess what I am?"

"Are you djinn?"

"Bravo. One of the djinn, yes. Shamhurish is what the Arabs call me. Your khalo always mentioned how smart you were. You were his favourite, you know."

"You knew my khalo?"

"Yes, I often took this form with him. I was there when he died." Shamhurish looks away, and I'm not sure if I can see a tear. Do djinn have tears? "I thought I could help him in the end. But I arrived too late. You see, my powers are not those of healing. Most of my kind—well, we are not usually benevolent."

"So the stories are true."

"Some, yes."

"Did you care about my khalo?"

"Yes, I loved him. I was his companion."

"And why have you appeared to me?"

"I told him I would take care of your family. But it seems I always cause harm in the human realm. You are all so unpredictable. And stubborn. I thought I could help Shaheed, help Chadi, help you. Alas, I was wrong. The chaos in this country is even too much for me."

"Why did you come see Chadi and me? Couldn't you have just saved Shaheed yourself?"

"There are rules beyond humanity's rules. I am forbidden to interfere directly in the lives of humans."

"But what—?"

"Never you mind with those questions, child. This is beyond you. You are better left in the dark. Your khalo loved you, remember this." He pauses. "I must leave. He is gone and there is nothing left for me here. I do not want to cause you more pain."

"But don't I get three wishes or something?"

Shamhurish chuckles. "You have been reading too many American stories, little one. Read the literature of your people. They will tell you about me."

"Mo?" Chadi asks, his voice low and weak, stepping closer. "Who are you talking to?"

I turn to look at him, and I can sense that Shamhurish is gone. "No one, habibi. I was just saying a little prayer for Shaheed. Let's go home."

✳

We arrive back at the apartment; the old building is dark without the streetlights. The electricity must not have come back on yet.

Neither of us says anything as we scale the stairs to the fourth floor. I take the steps slowly, breathing hard, my knees cracking and aching. Even after years of the elevators not working, I haven't gotten used to the climb. Chadi doesn't lean on me, even though I can tell he wants to, and I hold his hand, trying to comfort him.

"Do you think the rebels knew anything about this?" he asks with a quiet voice as we reach the second floor.

I huff and try to pretend that breathing isn't feeling so hard. "I don't know. You'd think they would have done something if they knew."

"They probably knew. They probably made him do it. They only care about the cause. No one cares about the actual people."

We reach the third floor. I am huffing loudly now, trying to draw in deep breaths, though my lungs are only letting me pull in short ones.

"No one cares about actual people," Chadi repeats as we make it to the fourth floor. I am about to say something when I notice Teta standing in the doorway. I'm not sure how she knew we were coming. Maybe our plodding steps alerted her? She has sobered up some, her eyes less glazed.

"Come here, habibi." She wraps Chadi in a blanket, even though it is still sweltering, grabs my hand, and walks us to the balcony. It is only when I touch her that I notice she is shaking a little too.

"Sit," she tells Chadi, then turns to me. "You, too," she adds, and pushes me into the next chair. The balcony is empty. I can't imagine returning to the room I share with my mom and sister.

She turns on the battery radio beside me to a station playing Fairouz, which I imagine is my teta's version of Aaza. "Allah yirhamo," she tells Chadi, hovering over us, and puts a hand on his shoulder. I'm not sure how she knows what has happened, but then I realize, people are dying daily. It is evident by the look on his face.

"I'll go get some chai," she says, and then leans towards my ear. "This country is so predictable," she whispers to me. I look over my shoulder at her in surprise, but she has already turned around, leaving the balcony area.

The curtains are open so I stare out at the sky. It is a blue so dark it is almost black, the colour of Shamhurish's hair, and some of the stars shine brighter than others. The sky the clearest it's ever been. A small breeze appears out of nowhere, a second's respite from the heat, but it doesn't last. I hear Chadi's snores, and look over at him, looking troubled even in his sleep. In the distance, I hear an explosion, far away, too faint to startle us.

SECTION THREE:
In the Heart of the Heart of More Garbage

Conversations with Arabs

Conversation #7

"I already paid for the meal."

"When did you do that?"

"When you got up to use the restroom."

"Why would you do that?"

"Come on!"

"That is something our parents do."

"That is something I do, too."

"I'm sorry."

"Just say thank you and enjoy."

"Thank you."

Conversation #8

"Why are Arabs so anti-Black?"

"You just went ahead and said it!"

"Why wouldn't I?"

"How is that poetic?"

"Sometimes the truth is poetic. Sometimes you just have to say it."

"Why is anyone anti-Black?"

"A want for power. A want of control. We think we are better, different."

"'We' is a false fallacy."

"What do you mean?"

"There are Black Arabs."

"Yes, you are right. I'm sorry."

"Don't be sorry to me."

"Who should I be sorry to?"

"I don't know. Black Arabs, I guess."

"But all we are is sorry. And all we are is guilt."

"An Arab's most powerful skill is guilt."

"Yes, my mother used the guilt trip on me last week."

"How so?"

"She said she was getting old and that I never visited."

"Did it work?"

"I am going to see her next week."

Conversation #9

"Here is the moment I reveal myself. Hello, it is me."

"Hello you."

"I don't pretend to not be behind these poems. Every word chosen by me."

"Of course. Poetry is about the self."

"I disagree," I say.

"You disagree!" you, reader, declare.

"Poetry is about more than the self!"

"Then why do you always use the 'I'?"

"The speaker is not always who you think."

"Neither is the reader."

"The act of thinking of you makes me better."

You say, "But you should write for yourself."

"But I am nothing without an audience!

I can't write in a diary, where I am my only witness.

This is for you," I declare, gesturing to a large party.

"But it is only me in this room."

"Use your imagination, dear friend."

The Good Arabs

Hassan hasn't talked
to me
or anybody
since the day of green seas
and we reduce it to absence
but they said
it's a changing in the weather
that signals more to come
and we're trying to understand
but this isn't a jump off the cliff
move
it's not a change
built over time
I can tell this isn't going
anywhere I want it to

we trade in seas for lakes and summon the ancestors
whose names we don't always know
'cause family histories aren't always recorded
maybe I need to jot down a list of names
of everyone who's ever walked me home
called when I was alone
ever told me I'm acting like my shit don't stink
because love is more than sweetness
when you grow up in an Arab family
when you grow up any kind
of working class

and any good Arab knows
you need to strive for the top
for the change in cars every two years

for the kinds of capitalisms we never critique
the generation before ours ate their colonial shame
tried to beg for mercy and only got a lesson in apathy
you get a car you get a car you get a car
but what about a lesson
in our own histories
our own urgencies
our own violences

any good Arab knows not to get too dark
because who knows what could happen
when you slip further away
from whiteness
and the view from the top of Mount Lebanon
any step up is a step down
for other people and yet

I'm saying we can't do the job right
the statue of Harissa
looking down
with tears in her eyes a miracle
but you're mistaken my friend, habibi
she isn't happy
she isn't well
ya Rab
I'm not religious
but I see our reflections
in her tears
and we're starting to look
a little devilish

underwater

we break bread, throw our hands up in the air
wonder when we'll next find ourselves underwater
our chatter rising up in synchronized prayer

this world is going to end in twenty years, give or take a few
how to muster optimism when everything seems doomed
we break bread, throw our hands up in the air

talk of foamy white waves devouring the earth, the salt like fat
stuck to the bone, surviving with strong and wide breaststrokes
our chatter rising up in synchronized prayer

what she says is *so what if our countries know*
how to survive, years of living the best ways they could
we break bread, throw our hands up in the air

we raise our glasses to our third world countries
empty of third world, only our countries
our chatter rising up in synchronized prayer

we all bask in the fantasy of renewal
that won't happen in our lifetimes
we break bread, throw our hands up in the air
our chatter rising up in synchronized prayer

In the Heart of the Heart of More Garbage

I would look up, if only to see the newness in the sky
but, clouded over by dust, the sun filters in
and a snake, no, maybe a gecko
trying to run away, hides in the bushes to come out
later at night, when the sun is down
people in their houses, the nightly power outage
a type of alarm
at the stroke of midnight, we sit on the balcony
finally see the stars for the few minutes
before some lights come back on
their generators working hard through the night
though some places
still shrouded in darkness
are only lit by candles
we cannot see

gathered by the side of the road
the dust almost settled
the no sidewalk
the no cars
the no others
the silence of nature
that is not silent but deep with sound
deep with movement
the dust finally settled
before another car rushes by
throws it back up into the air

hold the fig gently
but firmly
in between two fingers
squeeze, the smell potent and sweet
still warm from the sun
bring it close to your nose
to push away
the smell of garbage
repeat until your nostrils are filled
the smell
a protective shield
honeyed cloth
the mirage only as long
as fig season

cut it in half
the raw fig in your hand
reveal the red insides
scoop them out
making a V shape
with your index finger
with your middle finger
and curl your fingers

work through the insides
pulling apart chewy flesh

you pass one half over
tell them just how hard
to handle it
tell them precisely
how to do it with care
lowering the insides
into your mouth
a soft enthusiastic
drop onto your tongue
orange seeds
getting stuck
in your teeth

you see men throwing large black bags of garbage
over the sides of mountains
to places you can't see
imagine a small child playing outside
screaming in fear
as they rain down on his family field
mutilating the work
weeks of sweat and sun
weeks of unripe bananas
squashed in the dry dirt
falling onto trees, figs hitting the ground
purple breaking to reveal thick red
lines of ants in formation
a feast they'll bring back
to their queen

the *cigales* in the South of France return
like a fever dream
back from the insides of memories
barely legible
but the soft salmon of early sky
sun rising into newness
the darkness filled
with country stars
the energy in the air
so charged with *cigales*
so heavy with muteness
the twinkling of the stars quiet
yet so loud

it happened
in the fullness of my mouth around a mango
the yellow juices leaking down my chin

you tell me, I can no longer smell
the sandalwood incense in the studio
without thinking that someone
just had a shit
and is trying to mask
the smell

so the myth goes like this
the little Jureybon
"the little mangy one"
climbs the mountain tirelessly
no, wait a second, that's not right
actually, she screamed
from the top of the cliff
people shall call me Asaad
she said, people shall look on differently
people shall not throw things from my throne
peace will be present and devotional

people throw garbage
into the Mediterranean Sea
at capacity
the garbage shipped off to Russia
but not really
who will buy our garbage
when it's too much
who to pay for garbage removal
men fake companies
pretend to move the garbage
from one side of the country
to the other
take the money and run
the beaches no longer what they used to be
garbage in the docks
garbage on the buoy
garbage on the expensive beach
garbage on the free beach
garbage in the mouths of seagulls
garbage between your toes
garbage on the Sea-Doo
garbage on the roofs of old Mercedes
garbage on the hoods of buses
the summer so hot
almost sickly sweet
what if the day of garbage has finally come
will the seas part again
walls of garbage consuming the lands
she holds her prayer beads up
high above her head
the second coming
Jesus looking a little darker
than the photo hung in her living room

the smell of jasmine wafts into your living room
facing Champagneur
the smell of lilacs in the bags
under your pillows
the smell of lilacs in the alleys
and the Parc Ex sunsets
more purple than any
in the rest of the city
we sit on the balcony
and you tell me
look look, have you seen how purple
my purple heart is now?

my cousin runs out of the car
to the middle of the highway
raises his hand up straight
and before we know it he's gone
in a crowded van
riding away to the sounds
and smells of garbage

We count sheep to fall asleep

If looking is first, then love is just waiting for a chance. We count sheep to fall asleep but when the going gets tough, the tough take melatonin, admit to our defeat. We take the express bus downtown, which means we raise our hands and hope it arrives before the rain starts falling. We cram in to a small space. The man beside us, generous smile, smells like fish.

Hope is manufactured when luck fails us. The evil eye is perched on the edge of our bed but the nightmares still haunt our sleep. It is a shooing away of spite. Bring the dead back if only to ask them a question: *when did you realize you were dead and did you regret the war?*

That is two questions so they only answer one. *We regret nothing but the sacrifice of human life, now that we know what is on the other side.*

It Could Never Be That Easy

Once while crawling through the back alleys of Parc Ex
I heard cats rev up like cars
ready to pounce but—

Once while walking through the back alleys of Parc Ex
I saw a man touch the back of his child's head
with the most tender of touches
pushing the child forward as they walked sleepily home
and someone yelled at them to say—

The golden hour shone and turned the world magical

The protests didn't stop and the deaths didn't stop and the abuse didn't stop
but that hour of the day continued to show up
and the light brightened everything we touched

It could never be that easy, could it?

You see, this isn't the first time violence
has been conflated with beauty

A slap looks gentle in the raising of an arm, almost like praise
until it picks up speed, the wind pushed forward by her wide palm
and the red mark on your light cheek

mirrors the sky.

yt ppl think i'm yt like

i.

yt ppl think i'm yt like it's a compliment
brown ppl think i'm yt as tho it's a shame
i didn't turn out less gay

the yt woman on the metro
stares at me with plz die eyes before she gets off at laurier

while brown ppl in the middle east stare as openly: *who let u*
cut yr hair like that, asks a young arab girl
they will ask *how did yr mom let u*

& i ask her *who are they, they they* she says
but what she doesn't say is: *(if i cut mine)*
they will think i'm a weird gay (like u)
no, don't say it out loud,

arabs aren't
gay, no no no

yt people think i'm yt like it's a compliment until i'm trans
brown ppl think i'm yt as tho it's a shame

ii.

we go around the table being half yt
together, yr yt dad, my yt mom, our yt
family says shitty things, my fuck ytness
in me, my fuck dan savage's "it gets better" crap
or the yt man whose name i forget, the "face of lgbtq,"
says *love is all u need*, bet he doesn't even know
what half the acronym means

i'm here being mixed
in my mixed friend ceej's tiny apartment
as we eat samosas & i drop crumbs
onto his used couch, the room orange lit
pink & green lamp shades scattered around
the ceiling dark without overhead lights

we try to talk about writing
but end up talking about ytness over & over
like give me tools to move through it
or here's all the shit it has done
or i'm still half yt so fuck me right?

we say fuck the unbearable ytness of academia
& everyone at my job is rich & yt
& he doesn't understand my poor brown body
selling this expensive crap
& wonder if i can steal some or
my boss says *it's sooooo cool that yr arab,*
do u speak it?
can u say something?
can u show me?
can u prove it?

prove it, prove it, prove it

or *why they pronouns*
i don't
get it

okay i'll try
i guess
(she she she)

iii.

it's soooo boring to fuck in a poem but fuck

my body that is trans & arab &

fat & yt passing sometimes & sometimes not

& strange & hateable

& in pain & luvable & no & i mean it, fuck it

with care & gentleness, fuck it

hard & angry, no, fuck it

until i'm making small noises

i've hidden for years

or cumming obviously in yr hand

tightening, fuck & no

i'm lost & maybe not me

When I lived on Acadie

When I lived on Acadie, the cars drove by in heavy hordes
zooming up and down the street, reckless
with no care in the world, and me, a little body on a bike
not so heavy if a car were to ever hit me
and yesterday you told me thank God we've moved elsewhere
and yesterday she told me I'd rather move into a neighbourhood that's middle class
I was trying to give her an out, talking about race and gentrification
tall buildings taking over the landscape
buildings sold and brown people evicted
livelihoods ignored, she was telling me she was uncomfortable
and she was a white lady, and then I didn't give her an out
but then she left the conversation midway anyway—uncomfortable
we talk about race but not about class, you see,
and like yesterday six different gay men tried to add me on Instagram
thinking I'm a gay man and I said no, funny,
how things appear to be the same when they're not
and you know yesterday we walked down the street
not always holding hands, and yesterday
there was another injury on the soccer field
across the way and like yesterday
the police were outside the building next door
yelling at people to cross the street and like many yesterdays ago
I remember moving into a suburban house we rented
never could have bought it
the most comfortable we had ever been
or would ever be
I was six and my bedroom was filled
with Ariel, mute, her blazing
red hair windblown, a fascination
yesterday yesterday, we changed countries
more than we changed my baby sister's diapers

and that kid could shit, you know
and like yesterday I wore my jeans up high
and my hat down low and my shirt real flat
and some man called me jeune homme at work
you know, even after he heard my voice, like, maybe it's a mistake
but we're rolling with it, just tell me where the birthday cards are
he dropped them on the floor
and expected me to pick them up and of course I lunged
of course there was only one left when he tried to help
and oh he was laughing and oh
his wife was laughing, and oh I don't know if it was at me or with me
and oh, people give each other not-so-covert glances when they see me
but you know, sometimes they watch me on the bus not so subtly
men in Adonis stare at me even when I stare back
I thought Arabs had shame, I guess not
but I'm flying by them on my bike, and you know
I'm going too fast to register

Reading *Wanting in Arabic*

She says, "I want to curl into you, curl close, deep, and small,"
and I pull her towards me deep and small

Hand firm she grabs my leg circles me around her
squishing her eyes closed into tight small

Makes soft sleepy noises almost gurgling says
"read to me" and "I don't like candles" in safe voice small

Says "please gently" and "I don't care if you light candles" firmly
I nod okay   I light candles   I curl her deep(er) and small(er)

Hold her head tight in one hand poetry book in the other
reading *pomegranates quicken* and *blanket us*—how small?

Sleep reading: *how to say it takes to give us a long time?*
she mostly sleeping humming encircling deep and small

Humming to sounds that stick to her heavy
memory despite not seeing words but feeling words shrinking small

Humming at clicks of my tongue habibti hard consonants
lush S's monosyllabic mother tongue sounds short and/or small

I stop close my eyes several minutes of hard silence until
I'm almost sleeping deep breathing falling into her small

She half grips (/crushes) bicep bruise "thank you" so small
mostly humming mostly sleeping mostly deepening small

thirty-one lines for you

fixate on your words when it is raining and there is nowhere to go

*

the top of your head, seen from above, the birds fly, and one shits on you

*

when I looked up, I didn't see you sitting down below

*

the sun shines and yet we no longer feel alive

*

we move from one year to the next as though time is—

*

you ask if it is oum kalthoum singing and I say it is not

*

we eat vietnamese donuts on the floor while you pick at the dust on your carpet

*

smoke fills the air and we are told to keep our masks on

*

I don't want to choke what blooms so steadily with such a firm grasp we looked at each other only once before we knew

*

when the wedding bells rang, we didn't know who was in the church

*

you only blush when I ask you to talk dirty to me

*

fire licks the buildings and it almost looks alive, its tongue a wet dragon, a serpent's hiss

*

we can't fake it til we it make it because it shows all over our faces

*

so bored you decide to wash the dishes

*

when I held my breath you said it wasn't worth trying to hide, the garbage would still linger

*

maybe we missed each other on purpose

*

your intention is good but, sadly, you have brought nothing new

*

we forget to celebrate my birth and nothing changes the next morning

*

it isn't like others haven't loved like this before but there is something new in that look you give

*

we walk around and almost forget where we are

*

hold on with a loose grip

*

nothing more beautiful than a plane in the air before it crashes

*

it is days like these, grey-blue skies overhead, when i can't stop from falling asleep

*

some people say bathroom and other people say washroom

*

early sunshine, register the hum of your body underneath mine

*

you say no matter how many times we wake up side by side, it's still a sweet and slightly exciting thing, right?

you said your lungs were just so filled with fresh air out there in the woods

*

she slapped me with her plastic sandal and it didn't leave a mark

*

the pieces of building you touch are centuries old

*

the needle touches the record but no sound emerges

They Used to Call Her

the only disturbance
is the pounding of upstairs feet
but what if there was silence
what then?
thump thump
the only place I remember I am human
is in my bed, my legs start feeling numb
when I must get up to pee, when I must shake them

they used to call her
pretty little boy with the big eyelashes
wawwwww
on the street, so her mother put her in pink
until no more *boys* followed her
but the faint noise of silence
almost a buzzing
her mother wondered if maybe
the compliments were better
than nothing   this girl not so much
a girl but
the thick arms of a baby
the wrinkles so large
her mother pulled the skin apart
to clean in between with a damp cloth
as the baby giggled

but what say you
when everyone is gone, this poem is not about loneliness
but rather, the absence of sound
if no one is there to see you lonely
are you even truly lonely
at all

the women across the street hang their white sheets
from their balconies
against the yellowing building
scream from one balcony to the other
in Hayeren and the wind picks up their voices
across the large expanse of parking lot
landing the sounds gently, if not firmly
onto my balcony
as the musalsal blares in the background
Lena having once again lost
her memory

This Is Not a Poem

In this new poem, there are no words

you might think that there are words

in this poem because you are reading

the words you think you see but I pro-

mise you, there are no words at all, no

phrases, not one sentence, there isn't

an image of forgetting, grab your wallet

when you leave the house, or when you

feel absurd for trying to tell your mother

that you are poly, she says, does your

partner know, imagine you cheating

on your partner and then telling your

mother casually, inspecting your finger-

nails for dirt, gorging on the everything

of your desires. So maybe this is not a poem

after all, not the confessional you might

have expected. The fat around the pork

makes its way through the small spaces

between your teeth as you continue to

suck and chew, it is tasty, it is not a poem

but an indulgence, you are working on

turning the pork into small enough pieces

so that it can make its way success-

fully through you, to be made into shit

and get on its way out, but the fattiness

of the pork is your most basic pleasure in this

mouth, so you don't open your mouth

or say any words and like this poem, not poem

your mouth is not a poetic installation, but

the chewing is decadence, you have always

been a slow eater and you sit at the table

as your parents become impatient, your sister

leaving the table first, then your mother

then with a sigh, your father, do not leave before

you finish everything on your plate, but you

don't want the broccoli, only the fat

of the pork, and you are stubborn, and so you sit

moving food around, not in a poem, but at a table

in the kitchen and pick at the broccoli, and chew

slowly, slowly, until he says, get up and brush

your teeth and go to bed. In poems, there is often

this moment of reveal but in this nothing

is revealed, not a poem, nor a moment

of sinking into your chair, those moments are left out

out with the shit and the pork, unlike the ones filled

with fat and leaking over the edge, you say

not this time and hold it all in, until overfilled

you push it all out, and when she asks why you always

have stomach aches, you shrug

and answer her, this is not a poem.

Changing That Which Seems Immovable

The power was still a thing, then. To have looked at those
you deemed beneath you and raised your big-ass nose,
holding it high, heck, if I didn't know any better, I'd have thought you'd been
hiding some heart of gold, or the largest family, but for you,
happiness is not the wideness or the heart, but gold
in pockets, gold on skin, light
shining in your eyes so you put on expensive glasses. To have loved

and lost is not your experience. We think of ways to bring you over
but you never accept an invitation you didn't deliver
yourself. How does this make sense? Your breath reeks
and you guzzle more vodka. The expensive kind. I dreamed you would
perish, not violently, but just disappear, but wishes
don't always come true. In the mornings, we drink coffee
and hope it doesn't shred our stomach. The stuff that comes out of us
is only garbage when we've parted with the sweet bitterness. Somewhere,

there are people darker than you and happy. We try to fit this through
your chemical brain but it holds stubborn. What a challenge
to change that which seems immovable. All those hours spent
feeling guilty are better used arguing. The shouts only get louder and louder
but you're still not hearing. And now: the sea starts whooshing,
and now: the leaves start falling. Where are we? Nowhere you've ever seen
It is only in the absurd you'll find me running.

That last time was everything. We jumped up and down
and shook every little piece of garbage out of us. Some held on
like a hangnail you just have to chew down. The pain throbs
but there's nothing to do. The only pain we could ever face
was the one that had nothing to do with us. She says, just look at it
and we do, blinking often. When we see it flashing back and forth

through our quick blink,
we almost forget it is not our own pain.

The Tradition pt. II

There are too many debates about metaphor. The spectre I see is unknowable. What is life if you're living it? It seems like there is something bigger than us, something that is not a giant or the abominable snowman. The traditions we live in all come from somewhere. What is the difference between Greek and Roman mythology but the names? What is the difference between Roman and Arab? Atargatis was the chief goddess of Northern Syria, her body enveloping the country, looking from the top, unbordered and expansive. The Romans called him Dea Suria and the Greeks called her Derketo. It would be easy to say he was the same in each language but that is not how language works. She meant the most as Atargatis and gained her strength from this name. Is he a mermaid-goddess? Is he a fish-bodied deity? Is she real? Is she made of stories told over and over until they bleed any original meaning? Her territory, the waters of the Mediterranean, a mass full with garbage. She sputters to breathe underneath; she cannot wade through the waste. The goddess holds the waters close to her, enveloping those worthy in her salt and flesh. But her arms grow tired. The weight, the smell, the force of it weakens her, day after day. Leaking sludge and spoil, out in the ocean, crying for the failure of her body, for her failure to protect those who hurt her most deeply.

In the Lion's Mouth

We sit around a table at the restaurant, Arabs
are always sitting around tables, debating whether Arabs

we are, and if not, why hung up on Phoenician, this identity so far away,
culture we do not know, but if not Phoenician, and if not Arab

then what are we but a small country on a map, split not long ago, hands joined with Syria,
but split apart like during grounders in middle school, the weakest link, look for the Arab

in pieces, Syria, the larger chunk, left in the lion's mouth, with the lion's breath
dirty, keeping people under the weight of his paw, but he looks to the others and cries
Arab

so that unity can be pretended, a symbol, but what he really means is, don't touch me
am I not the brother under our common name Arab

if not him, then French, then British, but we must save those Arabs
if only from the Arabs themselves, if only from the tongue of the Arab

if only from the Muslim of it all, those of us Christian ready to gain the power
that trickles down slowly, only a leak from the faucet, dirty water, reminding us we are Arab

they tell us speak your loose tongue, if only to separate us
but we speak it in the streets, to neighbours, to those of us poor and also Arab

ya Allah, ya Eli, when at the end of your rope, when hope keeps you guessing,
like a cloak, like the last vestiges of a united us, surround yourself with more than just Arab

Can We Breathe When It Is All Garbage?

You, reader, are currently the only witness. No, actually, you, reader, are growing in numbers, and so we gain more witnesses. Hello, new readers. It is good. To be seen is one of our human desires, what we call universal, not totally manufactured. The structure is like this: one performs an action deemed moral, then another, then another, until one is deemed good. Some receive this designation more quickly than others. The pure of heart they say. We look into your heart and something doesn't quite fit.

There is no complexity in good, it sits soundly in our binary. We love a binary. The instructions are not always clear. There are so many lost souls. She asks me, *what are you even doing with your life?* The question is not unknown to me, and yet. The condensation on your windows grows and so does your anxiety. You try to fix it but the dehumidifier only works so well. The music you emit in response is beautiful and sorrowful.

It feels good to go along with it, to have you tell me what to do, to obligingly follow. A political movement is only one if there's a loud enough voice. The voice may be a blend of voices, or, physically, only come from one body. It does not matter. What matters is the volume and how many people can hear it. You try and you try and someone tells you that you fail. You fail over and over. It is you that tells you that you fail. You don't quite get it. The voice does not sound like your voice and yet it is your voice.

What is goodness but an attempt to push away the guilt?

We shovel the guilt into a pile and it begins to mount. It grows taller than trees, taller than buildings, and the stink is unbearable. What does it smell like? You are unsure but the word stink seems to apply. In some places, the fire licks the garbage. In others, it is simply ignored. When I arrive suddenly, I am shocked into smelling, nose hairs not able to filter it out. I cough, you cough, we all cough together, and start to make the same sound. There is no goodness in it, but somehow the smell is sickly sweet.

ACKNOWLEDGEMENTS

I would like to acknowledge that I currently live on the traditional territory of the Kanien'kehá:ka people and that most of the writing of this book was done on this territory.

I think it's not enough just to acknowledge the past, present, and future keepers of this land but that it is important to think about how each and every one of us non-Indigenous peoples have arrived here, in this space, in this case whatever traditional and unceded territory you might currently be reading this book from.

While some of us are the descendants of people who forcefully and violently colonized this land, descendants of people who were forcefully brought here, descendants of immigrants or recent immigrants who have come here out of choice or refuge, many of us continue to be part of a colonial project that does not acknowledge the trauma, labour, and pain of the Indigenous people of Turtle Island whose land we currently occupy.

I hope, in reading this, settlers will commit to reparations to people from the land you are on. I hope you will commit to education and listening. I hope you will dismantle your fragility and think through the ways you can be not a saviour but an accomplice.

To my dearest who helped me edit and put this book together, Trish, Helen, Shae, Lee, and Hunter.

To Helen, for going through this process with me and for all your care during this pandemic year (and always).

To anyone who has laughed in recognition when hearing the title "Nancy Ajram made me gay."

To my publishers Ashley and Oliver who made the process enjoyable and less anxiety inducing.

To all my friends and loves and family, you know who you are.

To all the Arabs in my life, good, complicated, and sometimes not so good. I love you.

To anyone who tries for goodness but ends up with guilt and shame. Keep trying.

ABOUT THE AUTHOR

Eli Tareq El Bechelany-Lynch is a queer Arab poet living in Tio'tia:ke, unceded Kanien'kehá:ka territory. Their work has appeared in *The Best Canadian Poetry in English 2018* anthology, *GUTS*, *carte blanche*, the *Shade Journal*, *The New Quarterly*, *Arc Poetry Magazine*, and elsewhere. They were longlisted for the CBC Poetry Prize in 2019. Find them on Instagram and Twitter @theonlyelitareq. Their first book, *knot body*, was published by Metatron Press in September 2020.

ALSO AVAILABLE FROM METONYMY PRESS

Personal Attention Roleplay
Helen Chau Bradley

A Natural History of Transition
Callum Angus

Dear Black Girls
Shanice Nicole and Kezna Dalz

ZOM-FAM
Kama La Mackerel

Dear Twin
Addie Tsai

Little Blue Encyclopedia (for Vivian)
Hazel Jane Plante

nîtisânak
Jas M. Morgan

Lyric Sexology Vol. 1 (Canadian edition)
Trish Salah

Fierce Femmes and Notorious Liars: A Dangerous Trans Girl's Confabulous Memoir
Kai Cheng Thom

Small Beauty
jiaqing wilson-yang

She Is Sitting in the Night: Re-visioning Thea's Tarot
Oliver Pickle and Ruth West